Mindfulness
Coloring Book for Adults
James Russel

This book belongs to:

_____

_____

_____

Printed on one side and back page is dark to avoid bleeding.

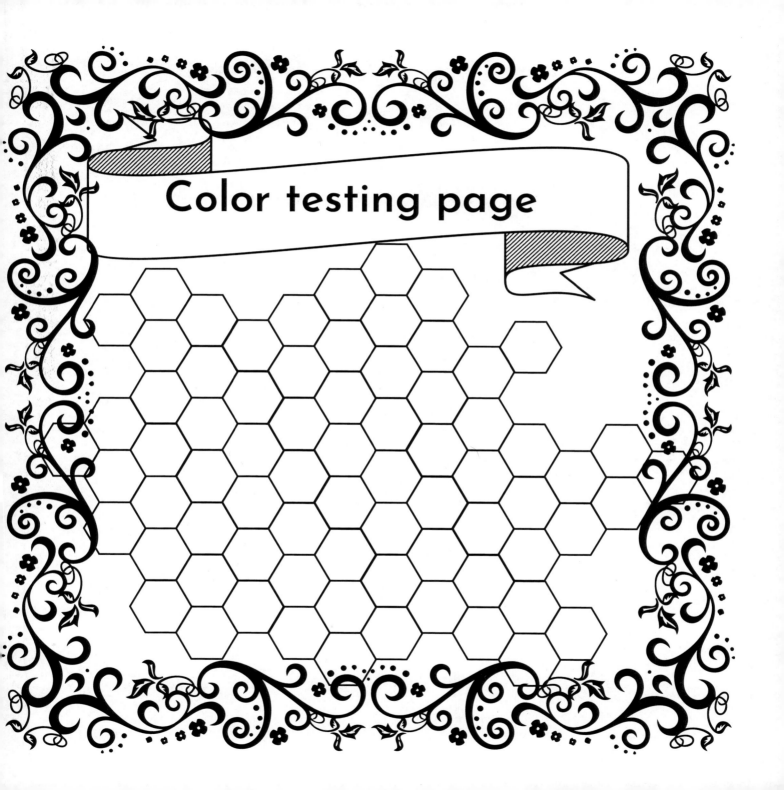

Color testing page

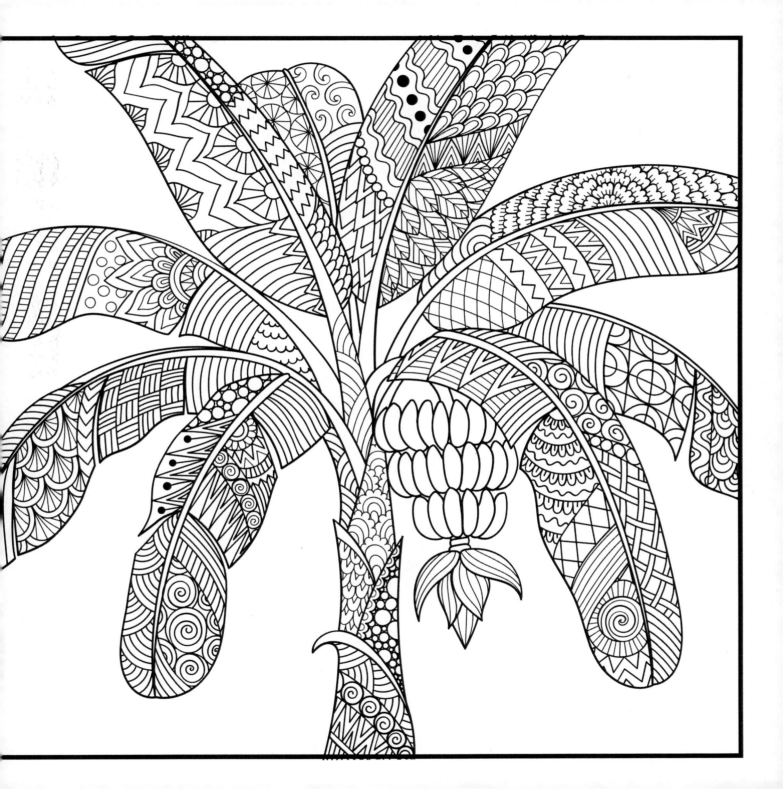

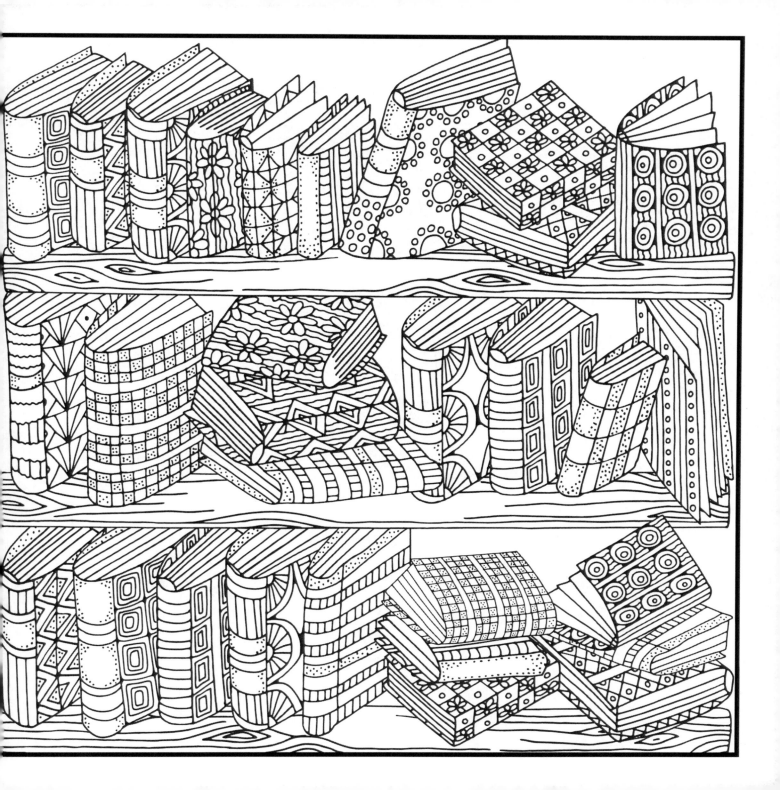

Hope you enjoyed the book. Wish you a colorful life as the book is. If you enjoyed then write us a review. It will encourage us to do better. Thanks!